Begin Anywhere

FRANK GIAMPIETRO

Begin Anywhere

Alice James Books

FARMINGTON, MAINE

10 9 8 7 6 5 4 3 2 1

Alice James Books are published by Alice James Poetry Cooperative, Inc.,
an affiliate of the University of Maine at Farmington.

ALICE JAMES BOOKS
238 MAIN STREET
FARMINGTON, ME 04938

www.alicejamesbooks.org

LIBRARY OF CONGRESS CATALOGING-IN-PUBLICATION DATA

Giampietro, Frank
  Begin anywhere / Frank Giampietro.
    p. cm.
  ISBN-13: 978-1-882295-70-8
  ISBN-10: 1-882295-70-6
  I. Title.

  PS3607.I223B44 2008
  811'.6—dc22   2008022169

Alice James Books gratefully acknowledges support from the University of Maine
at Farmington and the National Endowment for the Arts. ❦

COVER ART: "Falling Man" by John McGiff
COURTESY OF THE ARTIST

for
Cherie, Daphne, and Dominic

Grateful acknowledgment is made to the editors of the following journals, in which some of these poems first appeared, sometimes in earlier versions:

32 Poems, Amoskeag, Columbia Poetry Review, CutBank, Diner, Eclipse, Exquisite Corpse, Hayden's Ferry Review Illya's Honey, MARGIE: The American Journal of Poetry, Poetry Motel, Poetry International, Rockhurst Review, Tulane Review, Spire and Southeast Review.

I would also like to thank the following teachers, friends, and family for their help, inspiration, and encouragement: Ralph Angel, JoAnn Balingit, Lou Cox, Robert Day, Denise Duhamel, Frank and Ruth Giampietro, Debra Gingrich, Meredith Davies Hadaway, Amanda Kimball, Campbell McGrath, Robert Mooney, Jack Myers, Margaret Rowe, Mary Ruefle and David Scott.

Contents

I

II

I

Juice

I'd like to begin with my addiction to heroin,
though I never shot it, I only sniffed it.
(*Snorted* is so, what? Crass?)
Once after seven years without it, I talked
to an Italian ex-junkie who was still smoking hash.
Because she shot it,
she claimed that she was more addicted to it.
Instead of admitting she was right, I went on
about the purity of American heroin
while she repeated *no, no, no* emphatically.
I found her sexy in a big-boned
Elizabeth Bishop sort of way.
If I were Elizabeth Bishop,
with my history of addiction,
I would have to write a villanelle
like "One Art,"
but my refrains would be
A1: *I shared crack with a pregnant Dominican woman*
A2: *at the top of a five-flight walk-up on 109th Street in Harlem.*
They say you can let the arms
of the repeating lines
wrap themselves around you
for comfort. It's a great form for subjects
that might otherwise be a threat.
I wish I could say that my best poems
are written when I'm afraid. Sometimes
when my four-year-old wakes up, he's afraid.
The first words out of his mouth are
I want some juice. Now I sleep with him,
and I wake up to the request
nearly every day. Honestly, there's no better way

to slip from my dreams. I worry I won't sleep at all
when he kicks me out of his bed.
When I sniffed heroin, whole parts of my body
would go completely numb as I slept.
One morning I woke unable to move either arm,
but after a minute or two, the feeling came back. It's not
that I'm afraid to write about addiction—it's just
that this is nothing like that.

Conception

It must have been the night
I pulled at your breasts
till they were long enough

to fit into our pillowcases
because that morning I woke
to find the bed sheet had come off

the corners, drawing us closer.
You said, without looking at me,
I wish it was always

blue light in the doorway.
And just as I was about to turn over
instead of trying to gather
what you meant,

a stork ripped a hole in the roof
and carried the two of us away.

Another Poem Scoring 4.7 on the Flesch-Kincaid Grade Level Test

My wife will sometimes tell me I'm human.
She's one of those people
who cut to the green of the cantaloupe rind.
Critics say my favorite music is great
to listen to while staring at your shoes.
I'll never be smart enough
to be a priest. The best theologians never mention God.
In Venice they say that ambition is an illness.
On warm days there in winter
it's colder in the cathedrals than it is outside.
I wish I could afford to live in a place with a name like *Oberad*.
I'd have a cook and never eat simple carbohydrates.
It is possible to heal without justice being served.
A wound closes at the rate of a millimeter per day.
The government subsidizes my son's favorite cartoons.
Anger, in one, is a monster that continues to grow
unless you go with it to be alone together.
My son likes it when I draw cathedrals on his chalkboard.
Bong, bong, he says.
I broke a church bell when I was a teen.
I wore a gaudy Italian-horn necklace for good luck.
Once, in the vestibule of a train en route to Venice,
I stuck a safety pin through my ear.
In Spain they call the summer backpackers *cockroaches*.
This summer three Australian paralysis ticks
climbed into my cat's ear.
Now he sleeps and eats in the garage.
This morning, after saying my prayers,
I shaved in the shower with my eyes closed.

Vain

As my son watches the fish thwack against the side of the spackle bucket, I search my tool box for needle-nose pliers: A Phillips-head, an orange box cutter, razorblades packed in cardboard, and a broken measuring tape pile like ancient monument stones on the dock. Gills bleeding heavily, the crappie lifts easily from the bucket. It has swallowed the hook. I show my son, beware the fierce, sharp fin. We have lots more hooks. *But does the hook hurt the fish's throat?* he asks as we release it into the dark water. Struggling up the steep bank, my son snaps off milkweed stems. The banked willow tree hasn't an answer. I hold onto roots and dirt with my lying, stinking hands.

Skin

for Cherie and Daphne

My wife asked if her neck and shoulders looked red.
Engrossed in making a path

to the cement Buddha in her flower garden,
she lost track of time.

How many summers have we lived here? I asked. And,
How old are you?

Later at the supermarket
when my daughter whined for an apple, I caved.

Carefully choosing the greenest bananas, I noticed
her convulsing, eyes wide open,

unable to breathe. I yanked her from the cart
and thumped her back

with the force I'd use to test a melon.
After a long pause, she spit up apple skin,

pushed away consolation
and wailed for Mommy.

But what of it? Is there more?
More than instant karma, apology?

There is a synchronicity and swiftness of justice
that has to be accounted for.

Looking at that apple skin made me think of Luis Meléndez
who died poor and obscure in 1780.

Perhaps I'll always be as thick as Phillip V,
who refused to hire Meléndez as his court painter.

Or maybe there isn't any irony in a poor man who wants
riches and fame but who finally dedicates his life's work

to painting common kitchen utensils and regional foods
with a passion even a god would remark is foolish.

Maybe he saw the same thing in apple skin,
in the way watermelons split,

in ripe figs, a cut of salmon, the eyeless
socket of a trout head, cauliflower, cantaloupe,

or in his painting of Phillip V,
which he eventually painted over, with another still life.

Do I Know Berryman?

. . . this time, Berryman lived on Sanka and longed for nothingness.

— PAUL MARIANI

Berryman bought a phonograph
with money he won from a poetry competition
and lugged it all the way from Manhattan to Minnesota
by train — Berryman and his phonograph,
one of those old ones, *sans* electricity,
and very heavy, this large brown box attached
to one of those cumbersome horns — Berryman,
maybe drunk, clumsy, hitting himself on the head
with it once or twice, giving it its own seat on the train
even though old ladies lined the aisle.

Somewhere someone sick at the time
played the part of a sick person
and thought they could use their sickness in the play,
but coughed over everyone's lines. I mention this
because for two nights now I've dreamed of Berryman,
and of course the point of my playing the part
was I wanted to help him — like he needed my help.

My Brother's Head Has Turned to Broccoli

My brother is in the oil business.
I need to eat more broccoli.
My brother is twenty years older than I am.
I have a problem sustaining tension
over long stretches of time.
He is finally making quite a lot of money.
He convinced my sister to become a geologist.
Her head is made from the same
material lava is made from.
She gets to travel a lot. When she flies
she sits in one of those first-class chairs
that fold out to a bed.
I've always wanted to write a novel.
Once, on her way to Sri Lanka
she dreamed the plane fell from the sky.
Once, my brother told me
to treat honesty like an object
and keep it on the table in front of you at all times.
I told him he meant sincerity.
He said no, *sincerity is the tail of the dog.*
I've heard these days the memoir,
more than the novel, is where it's at.
My head is a cloud at the moment.
It always feels this way when I am hungry.
My brother lives in Oklahoma,
which makes me feel more at ease.
To get there you have to change planes in Houston,
the city where my sister lives.
Sometimes I get broccoli on my pizza
to make me feel better about eating it.
When my brother and sister fly home for Thanksgiving
I wag my sincerity like a tail.

Foreplay Pantoum

The back of my neck needs to be shaved again.
It's my wife who shaves it.
She's not uptight about things like that.
I do love her legs so.

It's my wife who shaves
her legs with my razor.
I do love her legs so.
She lets me use her exfoliating face wash.

Mom's Legs with Dad's Razor:
a picture my four-year-old son might draw.
My wife lets me use her exfoliating face wash.
I'd rather talk about her legs.

A picture my four-year-old son might draw:
Mom Not Uptight About Things Like That.
I'd rather talk about her legs,
but the back of my neck needs to be shaved again.

This Poem Cost Me One Hundred Dollars

Once when I lived in the city, locked out
while high on heroin and Ecstasy
my head resting against the gray steel door
of my apartment, I had a series of waking dreams
about purgatory in Dante's hell.
But now I'm the kind of guy
who spends five grand I don't have
on clearing the vetch and vines from my yard.
I'm the kind of guy who says *heck yes*
when invited to a wedding in Milan.
On the flight there I tell a fellow passenger
a story about my son's fear of the ocean,
and then nod *yes* many times as she relates it
to the Sermon on the Mount.
And when a beautiful Italian man
shows me how to tie a perfect
fist-sized knot in my tie
and then gives me his,
I give him mine,
even though mine cost a hundred dollars.
I'm the kind of guy who once had a tie
that cost one hundred dollars
and now has a story about losing it.

Ptoooey!

For I have recounted the time I was paid
to videotape a man
masturbating on a plastic sunbathing chair,
face down,
his oiled dick pulsing between the green slats.
And I have gone many days
as the French say,
having shaved with toast. But today
what suffices
is this thread
from you, baby spider.
Of all places,
you landed on my face.

Poem with a Misremembering of a Movie Plot Line

Yesterday my son asked me if I could make myself die.
I said, *Well, Dustin Hoffman made himself die*
in Little Big Man. *But that's a movie, and it's not easy.*
It takes practice and discipline to make your heart stop. Try it

and you'll see. So we both did, and learned
that we couldn't. I told him not to be too disappointed,
and that it takes a lot less discipline to make yourself
stop breathing. But, alas, once you pass out

your body takes over, and you breathe again. And though
I don't have anywhere near the willpower to do even that,
perhaps my boy will, someday.

Frankstory

History shouldn't be a mystery . . . Not his story
— CHUCK D, PUBLIC ENEMY

I have purchased an *Usbourne* history book
to help me teach middle school world cultures.
Everything from 8000 B.C.
until 1914 gets a single page. It covers
the highlights of each era with cartoons.
The first pages show archaeologists
studying strata. Looms
appear, 4000 B.C. A slave slashes his wrist
in Ur, is buried with his master.
I wish I had written *dates worn* . . . on the edge
of my shoe soles and piled them like layers
of earth. Would I die if I jumped from the ledge?

When my history is finally sought
I will write it like this—with careful thought.

Notes Toward a Long Marriage

Heather wanted James to read her by the panty liners
she left facing up in the bathroom wastebasket—
at least that's what he thought. James wondered
if it had been something Heather's mom had done
for her father so that her father knew when it was okay
for him to roll over onto her late at night.
But he didn't need this
to communicate with his wife.
So the fact that he couldn't decide
whether or not talk to her about it
was strange and troubling to him. In all other respects,
they communicated so easily, no secrets
about anything. Of course
it was he who had to initiate apologies
and the *we should discuss this, darling*
was his also. But as his counselor told him,
it doesn't matter who says sorry first,
just so it gets said. This time,
as he gazed into the wastebasket
pondering the gossamer stain while dribbling
piss into the porcelain bowl which she cleaned,
he stopped himself, moved a step over
to the basket and peed a little into it.

Me Spy with My Little Eye

Me and my paper plate of fried chicken.
Me, the hero,
  un-jamming the big grey copier.
Me, the escalator?
  Me take the steps.
Me and no more fifty-gallon fish tank.
  Me in my new hundred-dollar shoes,
and my, if me don't cut my hair just so
  my head looks huge.
Me, my head *is* huge.
 Me, my Dad's ancient, oily face,
  me like to kiss it.
Me fold clothes but no, no, no,
  me don't put them away.
 Me paying too much
for the teeny tiny house.
  Me asking for help,
cuz me can't get no cheap flight to Malta,
   me all stuck in sassafras.
  But not so with you, right?
 You're *so* smart
and *so* cool, but I freakin' spy you.

Lines While Waiting for the Water to Boil

The bottle of gin
is hidden behind
the box of Raisin
Bran. It's only a pint.

My wife doesn't want
the cleaning lady
to see it, while I can't
stop eating Cadbury

and peanut butter.
The teapot makes
an awesome sputter
as if the devil's staking

my chest for brewing.
But he's not.
It's just my stewing,
my tea with milk,
            and maybe a shot.

Fear of Takeoff and Landing

I bought this terrific watch only it's so heavy
it makes my fingers tingle sometimes.
I'm always lifting it to my face to check the date,
which isn't there. A motivational
speaker once told me not to look at my watch
and then describe what
the numerals on the face looked like.
That's the other thing I like about this watch,
it doesn't have numerals, just these raised bars.
My wife raised the flower bed in the front yard
with gray stones because it filled with water every rain.
Which reminds me that she's pregnant again.
I'm worried this one will be as hairy as I am.
A friend with three kids told me
she found her capacity to love is infinite.
I didn't believe her for one second.
She spent forty years of her life trying to leave home
then became rich and bought it.
Now she never leaves Denmark. She's afraid of flying.
I'm not; I'm scared of takeoff and landing.

Confessional Poem #783

I have dried my hands on my dog.
I have stolen the first line of this poem
from a TV commercial
for beer. I have used a cock ring.
I fear the art teacher at the school where I work
will use this knowledge against me someday.
I have asked my wife not to disturb me
while I write poems like this
in my Moleskine journal.
In the Bronx you can get a divorce
or incorporate for $299.
I have no idea what hookers do
when they are having their period.
So impressed by the physician's museum,
I bought a squeezable heart at the gift shop.
I have a son who asks *why* many times each day.
My cat's name is Seymour—like *see more*
I tell my son. Someday,
if my heart doesn't give out too soon,
my boy will pity me.

To Do List #5333

Discover all there is to know about pomade.

Consider the poet Czeslaw Milosz praying for the statue of Mary to lift her hand so that he might believe, as it relates to my demand that the cat utter a word—*hello*, for example—when we are alone.

Tell the cat I will let him in the house if he complies.

Tell the cat I will allow his ticks in the house.

(Who is Carlyle?) Read Carlyle.

Was it Schopenhauer who compared childhood to being an actor in a play just before the curtain opens, and being an adult to the curtain opening to bad lighting, horrible acoustics, and an audience of smiling demons? Find out.

Check if *Macbeth* is available on DVD.

Scour the paper for a local production of *The Tempest*.

Buy wood to make Dominic a pair of stilts.

Find the passage where God allows Moses to glimpse His back as He passes.

Buy a unicycle.

Make a paper boat for Daphne's next bath.

See the films of Kinji Fukasaku (master of film violence), credited with Japan's low crime rate.

Ask Dad to retell the story of the drunken Eskimo and the shattered teeth.

Throw away the remains of today's sandwich, chips, and sweet gherkins, left in tinfoil in a bag among several overdue books.

The Afterlife

It was after my thirty-one-year-old body fell from the ledge
of the skateboard ramp and lay on its back clutching
its knee, then its wrist, that I convinced the white sheet
of high thin clouds I was all right.
It was after I watched one chicken hawk follow
another into a wall of pine trees that I decided
if I can't be young in the afterlife, I don't want to go.
It was after this that the stain of sweat
I left on the asphalt disappeared.

Dope

The inscription on the barrel of the .20 caliber
derringer I carried in the front pocket
of my coat when I went to buy drugs
is as lost to me
as one of John Berryman's "Dream Songs"
I memorized last summer
by taping it with Band-Aids
to the hood of my riding lawnmower.
Of course I recall standing in a deep row of people
on the corner of 9th and A, waiting
to be let into the vacant lobby,
and then the thin nylon rope,
lowering its two cozies
from the top of the stairs,
one cup marked C for cocaine,
the other D for dope.
I recall watching a hundred in twenties
(a day's worth) rise up in the chosen well,
and a moment later ten finger-sized
envelopes stamped (that's right) *Death Squad*
come down for me. I recall
my light steps to Thermopolis
to order from a booth, excusing myself
to the bathroom, sniffing
a quarter of the contents of one
of my packets with a straw
and then sitting down to stir sugar
into a little cup of hot tea.

Indulgence

Here's how, having called home four times from work

and getting no answer, I thought my wife and baby had died:

Cherie is ironing her purple shirt on our portable board.

Dominic, playing in his walker, starts fussing

because he can't get the blowfish into his mouth.

Cherie moves toward him

when the ironing board suddenly collapses,

and in spinning around she overcompensates,

launching the iron into the air.

Still hissing, it falls pointy-end down, piercing her skull.

At first she thinks she's only burned

because the iron sort of slides down her nose

and mouth and chin as it falls, the way

pureed sweet potatoes slide down Dominic's chin,

or the way a pony slips in the mud on a steep hill

after a hard rain. My wife notices

the pain more than the dizziness which comes

from a severe concussion. So on her way back to the baby

she takes a short cut over the mountain of clean clothes

that I am supposed to have folded, and which I once believed

hid the key to my fortune in life.

But like that pony—please don't imagine my wife

as big as a horse, though if she were

I would love her just as much, size in relation to love,

relative too—she slips and falls on my son,

and eventually dies from bleeding in the brain

while suffocating the baby.

Now I come walking through the door and see all of this,

piecing together clues to figure out

what has taken place

just like you might come across a poem, or a painting,

or a piece of jazz music, or for that matter,

a whole genre of rhetoric or philosophy, let's say,

anything *that doesn't help you get dressed in the morning,*

or put food on the table as my friend Jay puts it.

It's like studying psychology, which doesn't help

or, hell, let's say worry—

worry and fear of the unknown,

fear of the uncontrollable, and the macabre

and indulging that part of you that indulges the macabre

or beliefs, then, studying belief systems—

and let's not forget irrational fears and hey, why not faith,

hell, everything and anything,

at first glance, apparently having no point at all.

Frank Giampietro, Poet

You eat with your fingers
when appropriate. You are a native
with an immigrant mind.
No one mows the lawn like you do.
The blue jays sing from your railing.
You drink your coffee black, like a man.
Why are your eyeglasses always smudged?
Because your sense of smell is so strong,
like your neighbor's dog, Rodney,
the Tibetan wolfhound—
the only one in Delaware, and such a smart dog,
so quiet but playful, not a jumper, very curious—
yes, a genius of a dog lives next to you,
Frank Giampietro.
When you work, people around you work harder.
When you're on the set with DeNiro,
DeNiro works harder.
You are in demand. You have a ministry.
You console the living, you honor the dead.
Your headaches are the price you pay.
You speak in cliché, but only when spoken to.
When you are sixty, if you try hard enough,
but not too hard, you will write beautiful—no,
accurate, poems. Some lines will be mediocre,
some genius, for instance:
winter has too many pockets or
it didn't take long for the skywriter to say I'm sorry.
And you may still have a problem
with endings, which may have something to do
with ambition—or Lorne Michaels,
how he's not afraid to drop a cow
on the stage to end the scene.

II

Begin Anywhere

I could begin with my father's strong right arm

heaving his shotgun into the lake.

This is usually where I begin. Or I could begin

with my half-sister standing at the top of the hill

looking down at my father's back as he hurls the gun

into the lake—not crying, just looking out at the lake

and the ducks on the other side eating the crumbs

Mrs. Dyer throws to them. Yes, looking

as a few of them—not too many—fly off

at the sound of the gun stock's heavy splash.

Or I could begin after the splash, with the ducks

flying back to the bread. Or ten minutes earlier

with my father not consoling, but wanting to console

my half-sister as she stands there, a shadow's length

from the doorway watching him hold

what's left of his first wife. Of course I could begin

with his wife shooting herself

in my half-sister's abandoned playhouse. I could

begin with my father carefully unlinking the gun

from her toe, or even earlier in the day,

with my half-sister having come home from school

calling for her mother in the backyard,

peeking into her old playhouse.

I could begin with her coming home

and not finding her mother,

the house dark and nothing cooking,

no light in the kitchen, no whir of the stove fan.

Or I could begin later, with my father parking

his great, golden Lincoln

having had an alright day, not a great day—

the high of having made the morning sale

worn off by the afternoon's empty store parking lot.

I begin with this because to begin with the fact

that my father has never spoken of this thing

living in me since I was the age of my half-sister,

or to begin with the lake which I grew up on,

ice-skated on—which the State drained when I was three

and did not find a gun,

is to begin with the idea that if no one found the gun,

then there is no way to begin.

No one officially looked for the gun, of course,

but surely Mrs. Dyer must have worried

over the story of the gun's disappearance,

seeking some explanation for it all.

Dear J, I Patched This up Instead of That One I Promised About Simone Weil

You, with your poems about women, would like this fact:
Simone Weil died of starvation because she would only eat
the rations afforded the French soldiers in WWII.
"After Eating an Apple, Core and All, While Riding in My Car"
is what this poem was going to be called.
I like to think Simone Weil would have liked
that I changed the title for you.
The first line of the original was about my grandfather
and his youngest daughter, my Aunt Jeanie.
He would spit in the dirt then tell her in Italian,
Come back from the candy store before it dries.
My grandfather never learned to speak English.
My aunt never learned Italian.
While Simone Weil was at an asylum she wrote
something about stars and blossoming fruit trees,
both giving an equal sense of the eternal.
As you know from our family gatherings over gin and tonics,
I like to flirt with the eternal.
I also like to flirt with a third grade science teacher,
ask her questions about the body.
She says it contains about a gallon of blood.
In the original poem I mentioned losing my wallet.
Among many receipts, I kept the line
about the stars and the fruit trees.
One moment I had placed the wallet on the roof of my car,
and the next, I regretted all
I had allowed myself to carry in my hands that day.

Angry with You at Bower's Beach

for Cherie

These curious fists of clay
I found wedged in the mud at low tide.

Or these odd bed pillows of cement that lie
along the bay's inlet and protect the homes.

Or the two gulls barking at each other over a piece of rotten
fish while their friends look on—if you were here I'd show you

the snail I picked out of the tidal pool, how it curls its tongue
around to feel if I am crab or bird or bottom of the bay—

but you're not—so instead I write your name with a mussel so large
the pilots flying to the airbase nearby could land in the C.

Death by My Son

Dominic and I are playing
with a bow and arrow in the backyard.

It's not a regular-sized bow,
but it's big enough. The sticker says

Not for children under 12 years of age.
I have ignored signs like this before.

He is doing well, considering
his initial frustration,

fingering the arrow to stay on the guide
while he pulls the string back.

We shoot to hell a cardboard box
on which I have drawn a picture of a kitty

using his street chalk (nothing against cats,
it's just that I can't really draw anything else.)

I show how you can shoot
way up into the air.

He is impressed, wants to do it.
But I grow bored

chasing his arrows,
find myself moving

firewood. He shoots one way up high,
says *Look, Dad.* I've lost sight of it.

It's going to land on his head.
I yell at him, *Run!*

But he's not listening to me.
I run toward him. The arrow finds

my crown, my skull.
I am dying slowly,

dizzily walking toward the house,
slurring, *Get Mommy.*

He asks if I'm okay—*I am,* I manage.
So he gets another arrow, aims at my heart, shoots.

Frankie the Haggler

Anyhoo,
'twas raining
and cold when we got to the station,
and by the time we did get there
those little *Baby on Board* signs
had receded into the darkness of their sleeper cars.

Ever tried to actually sleep in one of those?
Say, maybe we ought to have
a gander at the *other* blue thing.
Maybe we should spill another
bag of potatoes onto the floor. Maybe I ought

to rest up, for tomorrow
is another day. So what
if the palace is burning and you are sad.
Go sing thy aria in someone else's dense forest.
Chop-chop,

times like these, I feels like big ol' Saturn:
if the little chickens don't run and hide,
I eats 'em.

On the Taste of Horsemeat: Milan, Summer 2002

I have fallen in love with my sister's new boyfriend.
He is from Naples, and short, and I had to ask him twice
because I couldn't understand his accent when he said
he doesn't eat vegetables of any kind and loves oil on everything.

Cherries will not take hunger away.
A small coffee sometimes will. I want a coffee.
I want my watch which I left on the nightstand.
I want to buy a watch, a thin watch like I saw
on the man in first-class, made of silver with the date on it.
One should not have to make do with a mediocre watch.
It's saying I deserve less, and I deserve more.
I should have such a watch. In America we say *I am hungry*.
In Italy, when we eat, we give our hunger away.

A breeze is taking the bag that spilled the cherries.
To live with your mother in Naples is not so bad.
I miss the statues of Rome. *USA Today*
says drinking warm liquids on hot days is good for you.
In America it's not such a stretch to say I am in love
with another man. Facing the Duomo de Milano
on a black marble bench, next to a red-faced American
under a statue of a man riding a horse, I realize
a newspaper makes terrible insulation.

The archeologists will say the anonymous skull
of my sister's new boyfriend
arrived at the Duomo, circa 2000 A.D.,
bringing terrible news. I must meet my sister at two.
I must have that watch. The American, who turns out
to be British, says it's quarter till. Surely my sister

will be early. She has promised to take me to a trattoria
where they don't give you any choices except
for the wine, which I usually like dry. She is very sweet
and I know she will apologize for being late
and repeat that the food, even if it is horsemeat,
will be worth it today.

Please,

      Josephine Rooney, come back to Oswego.
This underwater scene has me bamboozled.
      The rock of happiness has fallen

      on my collar bone. I miss your *achoo!*
Sogni d'oro my darling *sogni d'oro,*
      for you I would staple my hair.

Makeshift

After, like,
hours at the Y

in Cobra Pose,
another week passes

without moving
to Italy.

But even if I'm not technically

in exile,

I wish to be kind—
to be kinder.

This size change,
it's temporary.

What matters most—
one produces something.

Is That All There Is?

This afternoon Frank has Peggy Lee to thank,

                                    Peggy & Frank,

        like a tattoo

    the sunlight reaches across the table to the plate of crumbs

                        where once there was a piece of pie.

Anti-Ekfrankcis

No more crap about the kids.
No more crap about crap.
Nothing about my sister, the rich geologist.
And don't try to stop me, I'm leaving.
I'm getting down off the couch.
Even though I bought a bird—nothing about it.
No more angry stuff because I can't think.
No more pulling the hairs from the inside of my nose.
Ixnay on the *oopgay* for the *izzyfray airhay*.
And I'm not eating anymore fish eyeballs,
not taking your oven mitt advice.
No more plus is positive,
or yodeling into the back of the fan.
I'm throwing my tongue scraper away.
I'm buffing out the invective
you scratched on my lenses.
I'm getting lasik surgery.
I'm going to talk more and listen less.
Today is the day I begin again.

At the Do-It-Yourself Recycling Center

It has nothing to do with being called a moron
while walking down my street by a woman in a white van
while on my way to get coffee at Dunkin' Donuts
while memorizing George Herbert's poem "Love"
the day I wore my favorite blue shirt and jeans that are,
as Frank O'Hara said, *tight enough so everyone*
will want to go to bed with [me].
Neither does it have to do with how every damn time
I open the door to let the cat in, in come a thousand bugs.
Or how in back of Safeway at the do-it-yourself recycling center
I stayed in the car and chased my wife
from the white glass bin to the blue, pretending
to pick her up with recycled lines,
the day she told me *I'm pregnant again.*

7 Spandrels

PALINODE

Today from a great distance
        I watched one of those giant skyscraper cranes
    swing an arc—it moved me,
        like seeing God's finger I suppose,
            the equivalent,
I suppose.

WHAT TO DO THIS WEEKEND?

Those zany country folk are making
      chili at the Saturday
market in a coffin—
    I know, I know
it's not funny,
      it's hot.

CORNUCOPIAN

What would
    my cornucopia contain,
            I think,
        what drugs
    what chocolate
what porn in my horn
    of plenty?

SMARTER THAN I LOOK

    This morning
            I shaved my face,
        as the French say,
            with toast.

INTO THE SPECIAL WORLD

Hello there,
        little chameleon
    who lives under the couch,

            eats my pimento cheese. I think
    I found your red harmonica.

BEFORE THE HULLABALOO

            Table salt moist in the shaker,
    wildebeest ankle deep
        in alligator river—the night is
            young, my little 8 oz. bottle of vanilla extract.

FOR A MOMENT I AM CHARLES SIMIC

The mouse turns into a beetle
                    and a worm burrows
into its abdomen,
            giving Frank, by osmosis,
a beautiful disease.

Tomorrow I Begin

Tomorrow I eat nothing but bean soup, or else nothing
but Raisin Bran. Yes, tomorrow I shall begin
my great Raisin Bran diet. No more chips for this guy,
no more French fries with mayonnaise,
or frozen wedding cake.
Tomorrow, I eat only things
I can pick up with my thumbs,
only what I can carry in my breast pocket,
only what the astronauts eat.
I shall eat only meat
cooked in a light vinaigrette sauce, only muffins
with one less yolk.
Tomorrow, I will eat only things I can slurp
off the lenses of my glasses with a straw.
Friends will comment on how good I look,
how much I've changed since even earlier that day,
how there's a certain hollowness in my cheeks
they had never noticed before. I will use my lighter body
to do good in the world, I will learn to fly, fly low,
avoiding radar. I will fight white-collar crime and speak
at junior high schools in poor neighborhoods.
I'll become fluent in Mandarin while commuting to work.
I will dedicate myself to God
and Man, offer up my new lightness to His Greatness. I will
have tons of sex, sex with beautiful women, of course,
but also with antelope and panthers.
My lightness will allow me to travel back in time
in the evenings after dinner. If there's nothing great
on TV, I will do it, travel back, and visit my larger self,
and I will hold him in my arms, but not too long
because he is so darn heavy,

and after I have shushed and rocked my old self to sleep,
I will return to my skinny living room. There
I will begin the diet of my middle period, and grow smaller still.
I will become what I am eating, a shape-shifter, a demigod,
a very, very thin, and therefore more confident man.

Poem Instead of a Meditation

I get as far as choosing a word to focus on:
it's *Grace* today. My neighbor has a dog named Gracie.
She won't come when you call her.
No way I'd give that name to my daughter.

Tomorrow will go by again in a whirl.
I'll wear my brown socks and black shoes.
Like is a feeble word.

There's just no way to see through the dark tint
of limousine windows
and no chance some nifty sunglasses
will be invented to do it.
A friend once told me I should be on Letterman.
Letterman doesn't have poets on his show.

I thought I'd read a poem inspired by church
at a stewardship presentation
I'm supposed to give next Sunday.
Then I decided to memorize the mission statement,
but finally decided to just increase my pledge.
It's the longing for belief that matters.
I'm going straight to heaven.

When I read poems about death just before bed,
my back hurts less in the morning.
I can obsess about things like computers.

In a dream last night, wires were central.
If I bring another wire in the house, my wife
is going to hang me. A computer is an octopus.

One octopus, two octopus.
Tonight I don't have a thought in my head.

I have visions of Satan sitting cross-legged,
his upper body just the word LOVE in pink neon.
Once a man told me in response to my vision
I don't dream and Jesus Christ is my savior.

When I think of people who say they don't have dreams,
I feel a little bit closer to a slug, my cat, my son,
and my favorite espresso cup that has a picture of a fly on it.

It occurs to me that there are no synonyms
for the word "dream" when used to define what occurs
while sleeping. The little girl in the neighbor's yard

is skipping numbers on her way to fifty.
Thirty feels the same as thirty-three.

I like to think of death when I first open my eyes
in the morning. I find myself praying
while washing behind my ears.
I understand from reading the newspaper
that it's an essential part of happiness
not to get everything you've ever wanted.

Our Siamese lost his meow this summer.
He sits at my feet listening for what the builder,
who's finishing my study, will do next.

My son keeps pressing a button on the remote
so that Buzz Lightyear continues to enter the atmosphere
of a planet where the evil Emperor Zurg is hiding, over and over.
I watch with him, uncertain of whether or not this is bad.

Meditation While Chewing on Some Skin Around My Thumbnail

Money has nothing to do with happiness.
Food is important, though.
My wife has started eating edamame
since making do with less.
My son would rather cry than eat.
I don't mind buying mangos and avocados
even though the prices
are absurd. On Sunday I drive across town
to buy fresh bagels instead of donuts.
A bagel weighs more than the average donut
but is better for your heart.
On Sundays I often have a heavy heart.
My favorite bagel is pumpernickel
because it's rich and dark.
My wife prefers donuts.
But if I get her a sun-dried tomato bagel
with light cream cheese she'll eat it.
I could be praying now.
Sometimes, when I arrive late
all that's left are everythings.
You can imagine where my heart
takes me for breakfast
when that happens.

This Morning My Son Dominic Watches Me Shave My Father

After a while he runs into the kitchen
to tell my mother I am making my father bleed.
My parents have moved recently
from my childhood house
and now live on the seventh floor of The Hallmark,
a building with a mighty elevator.
Here, the rules, made by the residents themselves,
say the men must wear a tie and coat to dinner.
Dad has so many age spots, half dollar-sized
moles, mottled, wrinkled skin. I had not looked forward
to shaving him. But he helps me by smiling
a grim smile when I scrape just below his lower lip.
His dimpled chin a crevasse, I wrestle
with his great jowls as they slip back into what was
his indignant but now wizened frown.
Dad is ninety-one and has become
wonderfully more and more sweet
as he has grown senile. *I'm sorry*, I say,
it's this lotion and my clumsy left hand.
The wattle under his chin is next. I say,
Look up and again, *Look up, Dad*
before he shows me his slack-skinned tendons,
sinuous as the kneed base of a great water-tree.
Finally, I shave the hairs that grow on his ear tops,
the same ones I pluck from mine. I linger there
and over his beautiful, strange head,
over the fine hairs that grow from his bald pate,
and think of his story explaining his baldness,
how the Indians scalped him—how
I believed him about so many things for so long.
And maybe it is because I have cut him so much,

but he is more lucid than usual.
He makes jokes with Dominic. He makes sense.
I wash the foamy muck from under his eyes
and where it has gathered under his ears.
Dad gets close to the mirror and tells my boy
to get a lawyer, so he can sue me for all I've got.

Jealous

Food meant nothing to Glenn Gould, he could go for hours
without thinking of it. Because of this, I suppose
I should like his music, but I just feel jealous.
I myself never engage
in anything food doesn't make better.
In fact, most of the time, I prefer just the food.
Wallace Stevens looks as though he was well-fed.
He was the vice president of an insurance company.
He said poetry *is simply the desire to contain
the world wholly within one's own perception of it.* I'm reminded
of my wife who made this most excellent fudge
and how she brought it to me with a cup of coffee
on a tray saying *chocolate dreams of coffee and coffee
dreams of chocolate.* Surely she has contained the world
by making it, and if not by making it, then by thinking
to bring me a piece of it with coffee on a tray.
She never writes down the ingredients;
she claims making food like this helps her
not eat it. And she just loves Glenn Gould.
Did I mention she can recite movies, scene
by scene? Sonny Rollins
could do the same thing with melodies: often he wouldn't
even need to hear endings to know them.
But that was a minor jealousy, and anyway,
doesn't a melody always end with the note on which it began?

RECENT TITLES FROM ALICE JAMES BOOKS

The Usable Field, Jane Mead
King Baby, Lia Purpura
The Temple Gate Called Beautiful, David Kirby
Door to a Noisy Room, Peter Waldor
Beloved Idea, Ann Killough
The World in Place of Itself, Bill Rasmovicz
Equivocal, Julie Carr
A Thief of Strings, Donald Revell
Take What You Want, Henrietta Goodman
The Glass Age, Cole Swensen
The Case Against Happiness, Jean-Paul Pecqueur
Ruin, Cynthia Cruz
Forth A Raven, Christina Davis
The Pitch, Tom Thompson
Landscapes I & II, Lesle Lewis
Here, Bullet, Brian Turner
The Far Mosque, Kazim Ali
Gloryland, Anne Marie Macari
Polar, Dobby Gibson
Pennyweight Windows: New & Selected Poems, Donald Revell
Matadora, Sarah Gambito
In the Ghost-House Acquainted, Kevin Goodan
The Devotion Field, Claudia Keelan
Into Perfect Spheres Such Holes Are Pierced, Catherine Barnett
Goest, Cole Swensen
Night of a Thousand Blossoms, Frank X. Gaspar
Mister Goodbye Easter Island, Jon Woodward
The Devil's Garden, Adrian Matejka
The Wind, Master Cherry, the Wind, Larissa Szporluk
North True South Bright, Dan Beachy-Quick
My Mojave, Donald Revell
Granted, Mary Szybist

ALICE JAMES BOOKS has been publishing exclusively poetry since 1973. One of the few presses in the country that is run collectively, the cooperative selects manuscripts for publication through both regional and national annual competitions. New regional authors become active members of the cooperative, participating in the editorial decisions of the press. The press, which historically has placed an emphasis on publishing women poets, was named for Alice James, sister of William and Henry, whose fine journal and gift for writing went unrecognized within her lifetime.

TYPESET AND DESIGNED BY CHRISTOPHER KUNTZE

Printed by Thomson-Shore
on 50% postconsumer recycled paper
processed chlorine-free